D0949002

Everglades
National Park

by Grace Hansen

Johnston Public Library
Johnston Iowa

WITHDRAWN

Abdo
NATIONAL PARKS
Kids

abdopublishing.com

Published by Abdo Kids, a division of ABDO, P.O. Box 398166, Minneapolis, Minnesota 55439.

Copyright © 2018 by Abdo Consulting Group, Inc. International copyrights reserved in all countries. No part of this book may be reproduced in any form without written permission from the publisher.

Printed in the United States of America, North Mankato, Minnesota.

102017

012018

 THIS BOOK CONTAINS RECYCLED MATERIALS

Photo Credits: Alamy, AP Images, iStock, Shutterstock

Production Contributors: Teddy Borth, Jennie Forsberg, Grace Hansen

Design Contributors: Dorothy Toth, Laura Mitchell

Publisher's Cataloging in Publication Data

Names: Hansen, Grace, author.

Title: Everglades National Park / by Grace Hansen.

Description: Minneapolis, Minnesota : Abdo Kids, 2018. | Series: National Parks | Includes glossary, index and online resource (page 24).

Identifiers: LCCN 2017943142 | ISBN 9781532104329 (lib.bdg.) | ISBN 9781532105449 (ebook) | ISBN 9781532106002 (Read-to-me ebook)

Subjects: LCSH: Everglades National Park (Fla.)--Juvenile literature. | Florida--Everglades National Park--Juvenile literature. |National parks and reserves--Juvenile literature.

Classification: DDC 975.9--dc23

LC record available at https://lccn.loc.gov/2017943142

Table of Contents

Everglades National Park

Everglades National Park

is in southern Florida.

President Harry Truman

dedicated the park. This

happened on December 6, 1947.

4

5

Conservationists like Ernest F. Coe and Marjory Stoneman Douglas helped. They wanted to keep the Everglades safe.

The park protects 1.5 million acres (6,07028 ha) of mostly flat wetland. At first glance, it is not much to see. But it is home to an amazing amount of wildlife.

9

Climate

The Everglades has two seasons. The dry season is from December to March. The wet season is from April to November. It very hot and **humid** during the wet season.

Ecosystems

The park has many different **ecosystems**. Each one has different groups of plants and animals.

An **estuary** is found at the southern tip of the park. Animals like bottle-nosed dolphins and hammerhead sharks live here. Lots of sea grass covers the ocean floor.

14

Coastal prairie is another **ecosystem**. Saltwort grows here the most. Marsh rabbits, green sea turtles, and frogs call this area home.

17

Mangrove forests are farther north. Mangrove trees have visible and strong roots. Fish and shrimp live among the underwater roots. White-tailed deer live on the drier land.

Alligators are found all over the park. They are amazing reptiles. Many people visit them at the park every year!

21

Fun Activities

Airboat tour to spot alligators

Bird watch to see many of the park's 360 kinds of birds

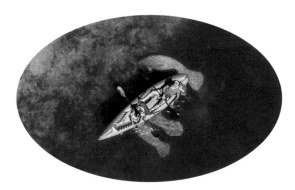

Canoe or kayak to get an up-close look at manatee

Freshwater and saltwater fishing

Glossary

conservationist – a person who promotes preservation of natural resources.

dedicate – officially open to the public.

ecosystem – a community of living things, together with their environment.

estuary – the wide part of a river's lower end where it meets the sea.

humid – having a lot of moisture in the air.

Index

Abdo Kids
ONLINE
FREE! ONLINE MULTIMEDIA RESOURCES

Visit **abdokids.com** and use this code to access crafts, games, videos, and more!

Abdo Kids Code:
NEK4329